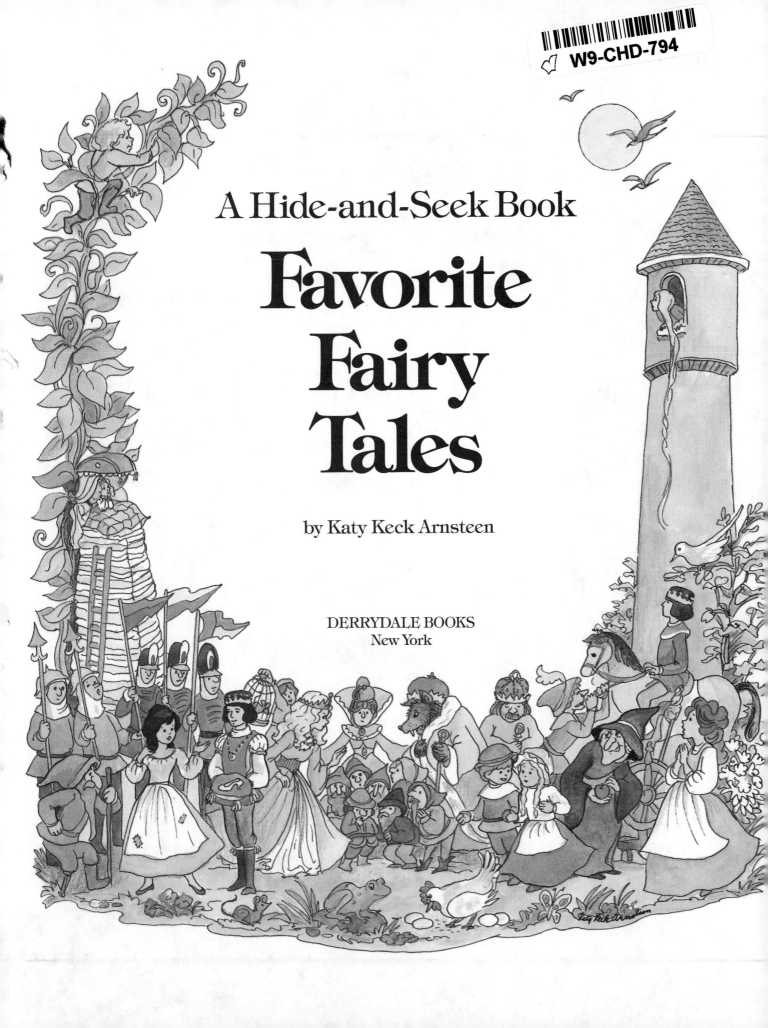

A Hide-and-Seek Book

Favorite Fairy Tales

by Katy Keck Arnsteen

DERRYDALE BOOKS
New York

Snow White

The seven dwarfs are hiding from Snow White. Can you find them?

Hansel and Gretel

The witch has lost her broom.
Can you help her find it?

The Princess and the Pea

During the night, the queen put a green pea under the stack of mattresses to test the princess. But the pea fell out and rolled away. Can you find it?

Sleeping Beauty

The needle-and-spindle that put the princess to sleep has disappeared. Can you find it?

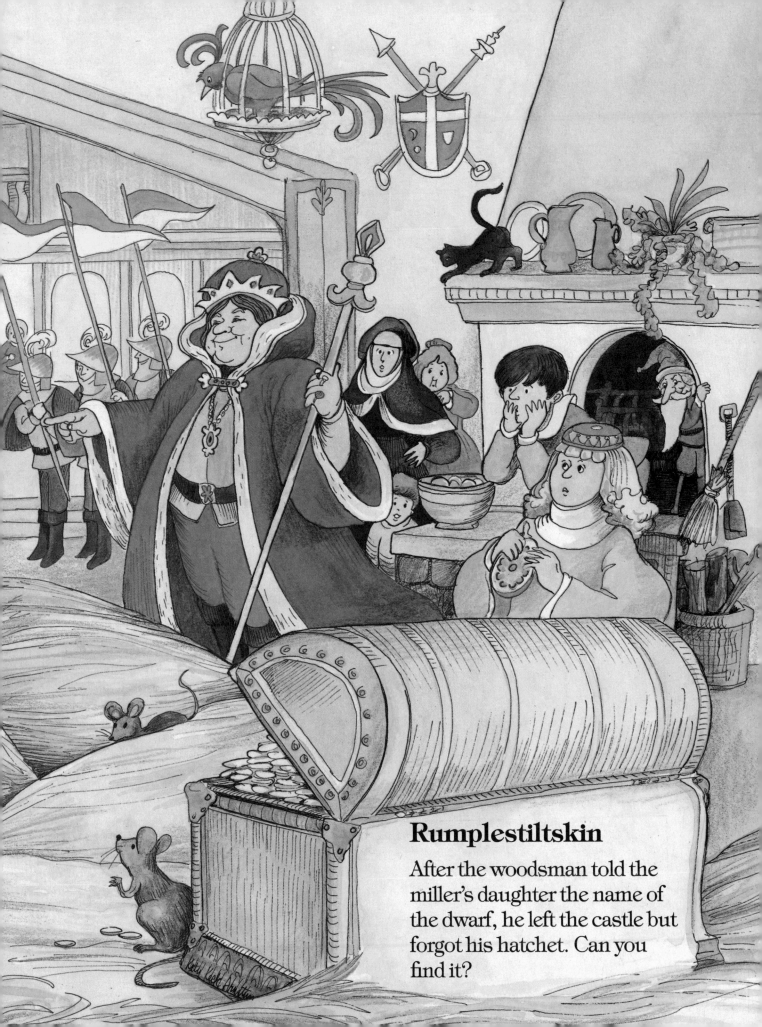

Rumplestiltskin

After the woodsman told the miller's daughter the name of the dwarf, he left the castle but forgot his hatchet. Can you find it?

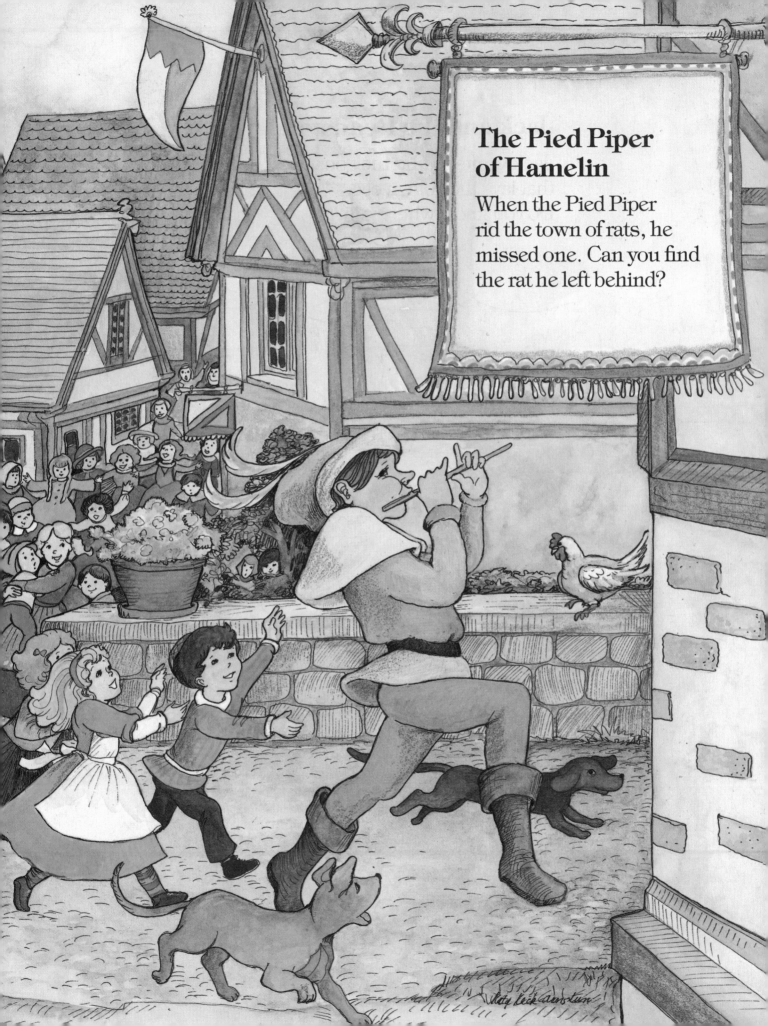

The Pied Piper of Hamelin

When the Pied Piper rid the town of rats, he missed one. Can you find the rat he left behind?

Jack and the Beanstalk

Jack wants to find the goose
that lays the golden eggs.
Do you know where it is?

Cinderella

Cinderella has lost one of her glass slippers at the ball. Can you find it before the clock strikes midnight?

Rapunzel

Rapunzel has lost the pretty red comb that the witch gave her for her hair. Can you find it?